SO-AJI-289

THE NATIONAL POETRY SERIES

The National Poetry Series was established in 1978 to publish
five books of poems annually through participating trade publishers.
Publication of these books is funded by James A. Michener,
Edward J. Piszek, The Copernicus Society, The Ford Foundation,
The Mobil Foundation, The Witter Bynner Foundation for Poetry,
and the five publishers: Doubleday & Company, E. P. Dutton,
Random House, Harper & Row, and Holt, Rinehart & Winston.

THE NATIONAL POETRY SERIES–1984

Wendy Battin, *In the Solar Wind* (Selected by William Matthews)
Stephen Dobyns, *Black Dog, Red Dog* (Selected by Robert Hass)
Mary Fell, *The Persistence of Memory* (Selected by Madeline DeFrees)
James Galvin, *God's Mistress* (Selected by Marvin Bell)
Ronald Johnson, *Ark 50* (Selected by Charles Simic)

God's Mistress

God's Mistress

JAMES GALVIN

Winner of the Open Competition

The National Poetry Series

Selected by MARVIN BELL

HARPER & ROW, PUBLISHERS, New York
Cambridge, Philadelphia, San Francisco, London
Mexico City, São Paulo, Sydney

1817

I would like to thank the Ingram-Merrill Foundation for a grant which helped me finish this book.

—J. G.

Portions of this work originally appeared in *The Agni Review, American Poetry Review, Antaeus, Antioch Review, The Chowder Review, Crazyhorse, Cut Bank, Field, The Iowa Review, New England Review, The New Yorker, Quarterly West, The Reaper, Seattle Review,* and *Sonora Review.*

FIRST EDITION

Designer: Sidney Feinberg

Library of Congress Cataloging in Publication Data
Galvin, James.
  God's mistress.
  (The National poetry series)
  I. Bell, Marvin. II. Title. III. Series.
PS3557.A444G63 1984   811'.54   83-48788
ISBN 0-06-015294-X   84 85 86 87 88 10 9 8 7 6 5 4 3 2 1
ISBN 0-06-091146-8 (pbk.)   84 85 86 87 88 10 9 8 7 6 5 4 3 2 1

For Jorie

Contents

Salt

The Spruce Forest

Half the Stars

Salt

Hematite Lake

There is another kind of sleep,
We are talking in it now.
As children we walked in it, a mile to school,
And dreamed we dreamed we dreamed.

By way of analogy, consider nightfall.
In relation to the light we have, consider it final—
Still falling from the night before
With ourselves inside it like ore in the igneous dark.

So I went for a walk around Hematite Lake
To watch the small deer they call fallow deer
Dreamed to life by sleeping fields.
Someone had taken the water,

Don't ask me who. The wild swans were
Still there, being beautiful,
And the geese lay down in the grass to sleep.
The shallows, now dry, were peopled with lilies:

Their poor, enormous heads reeled in the aquatic air.
The path was drifted in with gossamer
From the tree-spiders' nightly descent:
A monumental feather the geese flew over.

What happens is nothing happens.
What happens is we fall so far
Into a sleep so manifold,
Not even nightfall, whose gold we are, can find us.

Watershed

Here the land is tilted
Like a gambrel roof. The world
Slopes away from the Great Divide,
And all the people
And all the trees
Lean in the same direction
Just to stand up straight.

Even lies that lean that way are true,
Like wilsome pines at timberline.
When I die and turn to rain,
I'd like to fall into the distance
And stay awhile.

I'd be happy to be smaller,
Where close at hand is out of reach
And everything nearby is blue:
The denim work-clothes of the men,
Their axes in the spruce,
The spruce, the sky,
The knife that cuts the rain in two, the lie.

Fragments Written While Traveling
Through a Midwestern Heat Wave

1.
However lonely we were before
Becomes unclear
In our next loneliness.
All summer long the rain
Stayed west of the mountains.

2.
Underneath this landscape of sighs
Is a landscape of feathers,
One of blood, and yes,
A landscape of earth and trees and sky.
The soil of Oklahoma
Is leaving again.
Heaven is west of where it falls.

3.
Down here in the level world
Oil rigs make love
To the earth beneath the wheat.
All afternoon the wind blows hot.
The river is a piece of dirty string.
Like huge somnambulating farmers,
Dust-devils work the fallow ground.

4.
The real farmers
Disc their fields on tractors
With hopeful, yellow umbrellas
And raise white flags of surrender

Which keep the flying ants
From swarming near their faces.

5.
I'll tell you what the soul is made of:
More dust.
Behind each harrow
In each field
A plume takes to the wind.
The farmers,
At last,
Are freeing themselves
By setting free the soil.

Drift Fence

Whose hungry souls are these,
all in a row,
already lost . . .

and are they penitent
in shackles of barbed wire
on the bare hillside?

Whatever they were before—
that is to say,
whatever living pine trees are—

these twist and suffer.
The drift fence
drops off the hill

and shambles down through timber
without separating
anything.

It affirms the imaginary
line by wandering.
It reels from tree to tree,

lost in sundry
mystifications
until the forest yields

to pasture
and the landscape
opens its eye.

They cross the open country,
single file,
faithful,

each bearing
an undivided sorrow
back into the world.

Old Men on the Courthouse Lawn, Murray, Kentucky

You might call this
The far side of the river
If you ever lived in Indiana,
Ohio, Illinois.

There is no city
On the river's far side,
Just middling towns as similar
As printed roses on a widow's dress—

Perhaps you knew her.
She never moved away.

Nor are the old men
On the courthouse lawns in any of these towns
Any less like flowers
Since they rise at first light

And dress alike in overalls,
Gray shirts and caps,
As if they still had something
To do.

They have less to do
Than flowers.

They gather at the courthouse
From first light to last.
They chew their Mammoth Cave,
Their Copenhagen.

They comment on the height of the river.
They're too far gone to give a damn

About women anymore.
Tobacco stains bloom on the walk.

And now these men seem more to me
Like harmless old bees
Gathering the sweetness of the last, thin light
On the only side of the river they know.

High Plains Rag

But like remorse
the prairie grass
seeks emptiness,

increases
in its sleep,
gets even

with the fragrant,
stoic sage.
Oh, it is witless

and blind.
It cannot remember
what it was doing

with all that wind.
It waits
for a thimbleful of rain.

It populates such distances
it must be brave
but prairie grass

bends down in sorrow
to be so lost,
and like remorse

feels
so nearly endless
it cannot ever stop.

Three Sonnets

Where I live   distance is the primal fact
The world is mostly   far away and small
Drifting along through cause and effect   like sleep
As when the distance   unlikeliest of stems
Bears the unlikely   blossom of the wind
Engendering our only weather   dry
Except in winter   pine trees live on snow
So greedy   pulling down these drifts that bury
The fences snap   the trunks of smaller trees
If the forest wants   to go somewhere it spreads
Like a prophecy   its snow before it
Technology   a distant windy cause
There is no philosophy   of death where I live
Only philosophies   of suffering

Virga

In the distance some rain

that falls evaporates
before it reaches the ground:

a brushstroke on the air
that falls without falling, meaning—
the rain prays for us, in a way.
We call it a dry *spell,*

as in *enchantment.*

The Importance of Green

Small towns are for knowing who's poor.
I recognized her, the welder's daughter.
In a store she touched a green dress,
But she couldn't buy it.
The salesgirl scolded, making her ashamed.

That's how the sun comes through the open door today,
Still poor from night rain.
The road to town is a muddy tongue.

The forest stands ajar
And I could get up from this chair and disappear
Into the coldly steaming pine,
Which is like the next great philosophy
That will pity no one.

Its particularity is awesome.
The blue flower whose name I never remember
Joys through the eyeholes of a horse's skull,
A horse named Lola we kids rode.

Past the anthill roofed with mothwings,
Handfuls of elk hair like smoke the barbed wire snagged.
At sunset the invisible lakes rise and color
Like pieces of the biggest mirror ever broken.

Like those things,
But not those things exactly.
Interchangeable, let's say.

I could walk through groves where there are no paths
Until I was shrouded in cobwebs—I've done it before—
Like someone who lived in a dark cellar forever.
Like someone who lived in a dark cellar forever,

Needles resilient under my feet,
I could walk out into the sunlight
And tell you the truth:

The girl who wanted the dress doesn't matter—
No more than the dress itself,
Or green.

For Our Better Graces

God loves
the rain, not us.
Ours is
what spills over,
what we look for
that finds us:
innocence
by association.
Cloud shadows
feel their way,
rapid and blind,
over the face
of the prairie.
Pine trees
atop the ridge
row the world
into the dampblack sky.
God's mistress
rides by
on a feather of water.
After she is gone
her fragrance
is everywhere.

Water Table

How shy the attraction
of simple rain to east wind
on the dry east side
of the Neversummer Mountains.
Each afternoon clouds sidle in
just so, but rain is seldom.
Here what they call the water table
is more like a shooting star.
Streams that surface in the spring
are veins of fool's gold.
The water we count on
is run-off from high snows
gone underground.
The rest, the rain,
is a tinker's damn.

✻

My mother is favored
in being buried here, where she was born.
My father is from the east.
He tried to understand these hills
by building miles of roads and fences,
looking for water in unlikely places.
When we had enough fence
he kept building roads—
up canyons, through timber,
with axe and bar.
Sometimes he found old mining roads
unused in years.
Such innocence terrifies stones.

❁

Midyear,
if you drive on the pasture,
the grass won't spring back anymore,
so come September we saw the tracks
of everywhere he'd been since then.
To the rain it would have looked like a child's first attempt
to write his name.

Once he found an infant's grave
near a failed claim.
The writing on the stone
was also like a child's hand,
written by someone
who didn't know anything
about writing in stone.
It didn't say a name, it said,
She never knew a stranger.

Before the snow one September,
a man who lived here years ago
came to pay a visit.
He wore a white shirt,
sleeves rolled to the elbows,
and trousers the color of autumn grass.
He wouldn't come inside
or lean across the fence
the way a neighbor will.
He didn't care to stay,
although he'd lived here thirty years
and made this place from nothing
with his hands.

He showed my father a hidden spring
with fool's gold in the water.
He showed me how to use a witching-wand.
He said he mined for thirty years
and never found a thing worth keeping,
said the time to sink a well
is a dry year, in the fall.
The next we heard he'd died
somewhere west of here.
Then I had this dream:

❖

In the driest month of a dry year
my father took it in his mind
to dig out fallow springs
all across the mountains.
He had roads to all of them.
He thought someone might be thirsty.
I asked how people stayed alive
before he came here
from the east.
He guessed they must have died.

❖

I could say I understand
what goes on underground:
why all old men are miners
and children turn to gold-flecked water;
I could explain the weather,
like when the wind comes out of the east
and meets the simple rain.
The wind is strong.

The rain has slender shoulders.
The rain can't say
what it really means
in the presence of children
or strangers.

The
Spruce
Forest

Misericord

Out at the end of a high promontory
above the dim, oceanic prairie,
we built a little fire for warmth.

Who ever doubted that the earth fell from the sky?
As though it had traveled a great distance to reach us

and still could not reach us,

though we held our hands out to it,
some vague intention, some apprehension
occurred between us.

That night we slept in the snow
by a half-frozen lake.
I could smell the woodsmoke in your hair.

We heard the earth cloud over, clear again,
the low voltage of granite and ice,
and everlastingness

let fall the moment
like a girl slipping out of her silk chemise.

But forget all that.
I wanted to tell you, the girl,
that when I woke in the morning

small frogs were singing from the lake as if
we had become transparent in our sleep.

A Second Time

It was the year I cut logs for the new house and roads, roads like veins that let the timber bleed. You wore a different shawl each day. It was the year I shot the white mare, and her filly, equally white, refused to follow the herd to winter pasture. It was the year you left me the first time, before the aspen turned. Then it was the winter the sky couldn't get off the ground. East wind went down the chimney and filled the house with smoke.

The new house consisted of sticks and strings and numbers on scraps of paper. Facts are mercenary bastards. Spring was the fallacy that brought you back, but nothing in the world could hold you. The last storm we hauled feed to the snowbound horses. The white filly stood her ground apart. You fed that rowdy gang instead, those bluejays, vainglorious thieves that loitered in the pines behind the house. I wouldn't say you tamed them, but they flew down to you for crumbs.

It took all June to haul foundation stone from the mountain, to screen enough sand from the river for mortar. It was the year we cut hay between squalls, and the aspen turned early, their self-elegy, and the evergreens I'd cut turned into walls. You scolded the aspen outside your window for staying green when all the rest were gold. Now that you're gone a second time I already know what it's like. It snows inside. Jays swirl around the house like a blue shawl. Loud and bright they follow me whenever I go out—to the barn, the spring, even into the patient woods.

It's been storming for a week. The quakies are bare except for the one by the window, which is gold, in snow, and won't let go its leaves. The evergreens are singed with frost so that each is delineated, individual, each in its own doorway of ice. The new roof is half-finished. It snows inside. The early settlers here made houses out of trees and tried to live. When they starved out and moved on, they burned their houses down to get the nails back.

Explication of an Imaginary Text

Salt is pity, brooms are fury,
The waterclock stands for primordial harmony.

The spruce forest, which is said to be
Like a cathedral
Indicates proliferation of desire.

The real meaning of the beginning
Will not become clear until later, if ever.

Things no longer being what they were,
Artifice poses as process,
The voice is tinged with melancholy.

The teacup, the brass knuckles, and the pearl-handled razor
Resist interpretation

As if to say
That half the wind is in the mind
And half in the mind of the wind.

Speaking through the character
Who comes to faith on his deathbed,

The author makes apology
For saying things he didn't mean.
Little girl-cousins with ribbons in their hair

Confuse him with their names and are carried away
By laughter. Thus,

The force of love comes from belief,
Hate is from lack of doubt.
Paradox by paradox the narrative proceeds

Until half the stars are *absolute tears.*
The other half are *mirrors.*

Dark Angel

To the things we call opaque, the sun,
which has no shadow,
gives new shadows every day.

People fall
into this category.
Other kinds of shadows

are less popular,
like dry weather.
When an ocean goes away

the prairie is just its shadow staying.
Even the wind
makes shadows sometimes—

that's what snowdrifts are,
and why they can't lie down except
in the small lees

of draws and clumps of sage,
and why, up higher,
the deep timber fills.

Mountains ring these tides and swells
of sage and grass.
When the sun goes down

the mountains cast their shadows,
ardent nets, though sad,
over the shadow of water,

clear to the other side,
but not to be drawn
back in.

Rendezvous

During that time
There were times—
You may not believe it—
You, abandoned, and I,
A lonely man,
Would meet.
We took the result
For a more exact definition,
Which is to say,
Our bodies were too much for us.

I would give you a rose,
You would leave without your shoes.
It would seem to me,
Looking back,
Necessity wasn't so bad.
I gave you a rose, you left your shoes,
Still, there was more attrition
Than you think:
You forgot to tell me
What I never thought to ask;
I would wait
With passionate indifference,
You would not arrive.

Weather was mannered then,
In its uncertainty.
The well's ice went all the way down
Like a nail.
The line implied
By line of sight

Was a delirious streamer
Fixed to us.
We were also something like a nail,
One that fixed
A significant location,
Though not in itself
Significant.

To See the Stars in Daylight

You have to go down
in a deep mine-shaft or a well,

down where you can imagine the incomparable
piety of the schoolbus,
the wherewithal of bees,

down where you can be a drawer full of dust
as night comes on under full sail,

and the smooth rain,
in its beautiful armor,
stands by forever.

I believe
there's a fiddle in the wings

whose music is full of holes
and principles beyond reason.
It binds our baleful human hearts

to wristwatches and planets,
it breaks into fragments which are not random.

The girl in the white dress kneels by the riverbank
and, like the willow, leans
and trails her fingers in the current.

She doesn't know about the damsel fly, exquisitely blue,
that has fallen asleep on her pillow.

Girl on the Pier

The pier is less like a bridge than a well,
Since it leads to water.

Bridges are for crossing in pairs.
Standing alone at the end of the pier

The girl is brave and fragile, more beautiful
At this moment than anything in the world.

Her salty handkerchief wants to be a sail.
The ship is long since out of sight;

The distance where she looks for it
Whiles away in blue.

How I would like to hold her,
To bring her back from the end of the pier!

Analogy breaks down when it comes to tears.
When it comes to oceans bridges don't prevail.

The girl thinks the pier is a bridge that fails.
The waves, she thinks, must be ideal

Since they break behind her on the actual shore:
That's the genius of the pier.

The girl looks down at her handkerchief
To find a single eyelash

Whereby she makes a sentimental wish,
A wish that water seeks to fulfill,

Whether salt or fresh,
In the wave or the well.

Practice

The world arrived
so carefully packed
in time,
in time to open,
it could have been
God's parachute.
We booby-trapped it.
God, you will remember
from the Old Testament,
was a terrorist.
Now He's a generalization.
We've taken to scaring ourselves.
We scare the ozone layer.
But today, still spinning
around the world's axis,
which is imaginary,
I was permitted to walk home
again through writhing spring.
Leafy things and flowers
in earnest everywhere,
ignoring fear.
If it was anything

it was a garden.
Then, by the gymnasium
I saw a girl
in a green leotard with long sleeves.
She wasn't just any girl,
she was a dancer,
which is to say only
she didn't regret

her body.
She moved in it
and it moved.
She spun herself around.
She wasn't dancing, exactly,
more like she was practicing a dance,
getting the moves right,
which moved me
even more.

Sure I wanted her,
but I stood quietly
as she practiced dancing
alone, without music,
and then I continued on.
It wouldn't have been a good thing
to interrupt that solitude,
identical with her body,
or risk frightening her
with speech.

Scrimshaw

There you are,
end of sorrow,
so abstract
in your black dress,

so effortlessly
formal.

You trail your left hand
down the bannister
and avoid the light
from the chandelier.

How like an actual
girl you are,
drawing near,

how your bearing
requires
the scrimshaw fan you carry.

When you open it
to conceal a hint
of color on your cheek,
it reveals

the arctic distances
of bone,

and sailors setting out
in tiny hopeful ships.

Leaving the Tilted City

Love, if you exist
don't tell anyone.

Murderers line the streets like glass doors,
and merciful lies aren't wrong.

We'll tell them I'm the inspector of lightning
or a failed puppeteer.

They won't know the difference
if we leave the tilted city,

if we float downriver
on a raft of mandolins.

I remember believing in you.
I believed you were there to answer.

But that was before
I had ever touched you.

Sempiternal

Out at sea the sun
was shining,
but only in one place,
like a silver dish
on the rain-darkened water.
A single whale,
sated with love,
steaming north from Baja,
was too distant to see,
but we could

see where he was breathing:
a tree made of water
and filled with silver light
appeared on the air,
already falling,
and after a whale-breath,
reappeared—
the self-same form—
a little farther
north each time.

After the Papago

for Ruth Underhill

I've done it now.
I've come back where something good is my desire.
And now, though at first I didn't know,
It has happened.

I like it and gather it up.

I crawled off and I couldn't stand it.
I thought of my house and I went there.
When I saw my house I couldn't stand it.
I turned around and talked to myself.
I remembered you.

The water runs quickly.
The water plants grow.

I like it and gather it up.

Small trout are swept backward downstream.

There is my wind and it reaches me.
So very nicely and wetly it blows.

There is my cloud and it reaches me
So very nicely and wetly.

I like it and gather it up.

Now I turn homeward
On the homeward road.

Half
the
Stars

A Poem from the Edge of America

There are ways of finding things, like stumbling on them.
Or knowing what you're looking for.
A miss is as good as a mile.
There are ways to put the mind at ease, like dying,
But first you have to find a place to lie down.

Once, in another life, I was a boy in Wyoming.
I called freedom home.
I had walked a long time into a high valley.
A river ran through it. It was late,
And I was looking for a place to lie down,

Which didn't keep me from stumbling
On something, believe me, I never wanted to find.
It was only the skeleton of someone's horse,
Saddled and bridled and tied to a tree.
When I woke in the morning it was next to me.

The rider must have wandered off, got turned around
And lost. It must have been winter.
The horse starved by the tree.
When we say, *what a shame*, whose shame do we mean?
In earnest of stability water often rages,

But rivers find their banks again, in earnest of the sea.
This ocean I live on can't hold still.
I want to go home to Wyoming and lie down
Like that river I remember with a valley to flow in,
The ocean half a continent away.

The horse I spoke of isn't a reason,
Although it might be why.

Above Half Moon

Not even a bird can sleep in thin air, a thousand feet higher than the highest trees on Half Moon Pass, where summer lasts a month or less, and the rest is just high wind and low clouds, like now, a landscape removed to the sky. Even the snow can't stand it here, it jumps at the first breeze and feathers down to the timber.

A single drift, a crescent, naps in the lee of the cabin. Whoever built this claim a hundred years ago must have been a lunatic, or driven. He chipped out his mine-shaft, one man's monument to hard luck, an obelisk of air pointing straight down. Maybe he counted on Holy Cross Mountain for grace. May be he just liked being alone in the sky.

The logs still show where his adze bit in. He fitted them with broad axe and bucksaw, and pegged them together the way they used to make the hulls of ships, but this was built with wind in mind and too much empty sky around. The walls are double, pinestraw in between: a house inside a house with double-shuttered windows, a flower made of timber, whose trail down is a crooked stem.

How he hauled his timber up the talus slope, a mile of switchbacks, was, I'd guess, a mule. He hauled the logs a log at a time. Who knows how he got that woodstove home, or what he thought of moonless nights awash in stars, or if the kerosene light seemed cold and far away. He must have hauled his firewood too, and melted snow sometimes for water.

I guess there was no place to go from here. The door opens on a view of the mountain when the weather is clear or the clouds are down below. The lake below the mountain is called The Bowl of Tears. I don't know, maybe he was crazy and wanted to be rich. Maybe he wanted to be alone with God. You can see where he nailed tin cans hammered flat and old boot soles over the cracks in the door.

Anthropology

Remember the night you got drunk
and shot the roses?
You were a perfect stranger, Father,
even my bad sister cried.

Some other gravity,
not death or luck,
drew fish out of the sea
and started them panting.

The fish became a man.
The archer's bow became a violin.
I remember the night you searched the sofa
for change

and wept on the telephone.
Some other gravity,
not time or entropy,
pulled the knife down for centuries.

The archers dropped their bows,
harmless as pine needles in the snow.
The knife became a plow
and entered the earth, Father.

Later it became a boat
and some other things—
It isn't a dream but it takes a long time,
for the archer's bow to become a violin.

Upland Birds

I dreamed a tall spruce grove
planted in deep earth.
The branches were full of secret birds
that sang together as well as separately.

When I was young
we hunted wood grouse in deep spruce groves.
We called them fool hens.
We killed them with rocks.

They couldn't fly away very far.
Sometimes they were so confused
they walked right up to us
or perched in easy range and watched.

The kind of grouse we found on the prairie
was a different story.
Living far from trees had made them wary.
They watched the ground for shadows of wings.

They watched the horizon for coyotes and men.
In winter I could find them
among the shacks of an abandoned ranch
that was like a shipwreck on the plains.

It was the only windbreak
for miles of open space.
They'd wait until I was barely close
before they exploded into the sky and drifted

a quarter-mile or so downwind.
And I ran after them.

Each time they'd fly, not far,
before I came too near,

and I ran after them again and again,
until I was too tired to follow anymore,
and miles from home or any tree,
under the blue, enormous sky.

Above timberline we tried to catch ptarmigan.
In summer they are the color of the rocks
and tundra grass they lie down among.
In winter they are white

and lie down in the snow.
We hardly ever saw them,
but when we did we caught them in our hands
and let them go.

On Sharing What We Never Had

Ray, my neighbor, was born in a claim shack that didn't belong to anyone, but Ray owned the whole mountain if owning means you don't have to share. He was twelve years old before he ever saw a stranger: a peg-legged fisherman working the ponds on Nigger Bob Creek. Ray sneaked up behind a tree and watched till dark.

On the county road the tourists stop to marvel at a large balsam tree, an impossible tire girdling its trunk. That tire went flat in 1940, when Ray and Margie had just been married. Margie said it was a hell of a note. Ray threw the tire over a sapling, not thinking how someday, now, it would fit snug as a ring.

As I drive up to the house, Margie is hanging glass bottles of sugar-water under the eaves. Hummingbirds lace the air around her like a gust of leaves. They perch on her outstretched fingers like jewelry.

Ray and I take fly rods and a fifth of rye up Nigger Bob Creek. They've sold this ground to developers, the ponds are mostly silted-in. We weren't fishing anyway. Why should it hurt to share what we never had a right to? On the way home Ray stops the truck by the balsam tree. He says he still can't figure out why he did that, why a man would do such a thing. He eases the truck back into the road and asks did I ever wonder who Nigger Bob was.

Sara

Sara stays at home.
Her looks are plain.
She paints somber landscapes with sleeping horses.
She hears voices.

She's going to stop living later this afternoon.

Now she's painting the uncut hay waiting in the meadow,
that her father and brothers used to mow
when they were alive.

Sara knows from observation
how it is with trees—without a forest
they can't go on.
Her mother tells Sara not to paint so sad.

Look, she says, standing at the bay window,
cleaning the glass with a white cloth,

It's beautiful, not sad!
The walls of the house are covered with Sara's landscapes.
It's like not having any walls.

The sun is hot on the brim of her straw hat,
and the valley can't imagine itself
without her.
She paints the hay barn, leaning a little,

the snowfence, also leaning,
the pines behind the house and barn

a sadder green than pine trees are.

The house, from the outside, is plain.
Sara paints her mother standing at the window,

a white cloth against the glass.

Whistle

This morning I hoofed out. It was cold as two sticks.
There should be snow by now.
The ground has had enough. It's anvil-hard.
It won't be accepting any more death till spring.

Among patches of red earth abraded by wind
Weedstalks and grass stems and crystalline leaves
Wait to lower themselves back down.
I walked home without leaving tracks, like an angel.

Burnt-out, winterbare, this handbasket
Needs a covering of snow. There should be snow by now.
Earth revealed like this demands a dignity
That was never in us. White veil, black veil,

The bride's, the widow's countenance,
The faces of the dead-by-violent-causes,
It's bad to gaze upon them.
A lace of snow is needed here, permission

To forget.
The creek below the spring whistles under its breath,
Just making believe.

Almost Noon

The water, you remember,
Was so cold it took our breath
Until we laughed. The sun didn't shine down there at all
Except at noon. You remember. No one
Ever took your picture there, but this one:
Granite walls, deep water, cedar, your favorite spot,
Where I threw your ashes into the falls.

I like the hat you're wearing, Father's straw one,
Though it casts your eyes in shadow.
I can tell what time it is
By how much of you is missing.
The children can go swimming now.

Sometimes things happen this way,
And I can't talk about it.
There are smaller, darker shadows gathered in your ears.
They are planning an invasion. Listen,
You can't even hear them.
You are turning to the camera, saying yes.

Still Here

The light is trying trying to be tangible
When it strikes the angle
Of a good blade on the wheel.
Some high silky clouds tune up
For a real Western sunset.
The shadows of things would be alarming
If you didn't know
They were only shadows.
The horses drift in from pasture
With their heads down.
Since horses don't pray they must be grazing.
Lost in tenderness,
They could be, already, in another life.
Ray drives up so slowly,
An old man in a red pick-up,
He hardly raises any dust.
He likes leaving things the way they are.
The surface of the earth, let's face it,
Is abrasive.
Things get smaller
Even when they grow.
We sit out back on the cooler, facing west,
With a jug between us.
Ray lifts a tumbler half-full of rum.
Right now I'm a millionaire,
He says and tips it back.
The horses drift off, out of sight
Behind some hills,
The world surrenders its details,
But we're still here,
Riding the edge of failing light—
Steel-dust in a swirl.

Snowherd

The industry of flowers
Is dying young.
My friend Ray, I'm afraid, is gone.
His crook was a shovel,
His flock was water.
Winter his flock was snow,
So Ray built snowfences along the ditches
And shoveled in spring
To make them run.
Ray was a water engineer,
Which means
He filled the reservoir
For the ranchers
On the prairie.

Upwind, downstream,
Almost just in time,
Ray just wanted to help someone
By building a bridge
Across a ditch
Or clearing a neighbor's winter road.
(He even gathered mountain phlox,
Which looks like melting snow,
For a certain widow's windowbox.)
It's hard to be happy
In such dry country.
Ray filled the reservoir
For the ranches on the prairie,
Where otherwise only weeds would grow.

Up the mountain, early spring,
He shouldered his shovel

Like a single, useless wing.
Under the grass was the last thing he wanted,
Which means he wanted it at last.
All the ditches filled with snow,
The headgates froze.
Moth wings drifted
On windowsills,
And the ants came along in single file.
Each one shouldered a wing
And climbed the window into the sky,
As if to show us humility,
The science of living on.

Shadow-Casting

This boy's father dies.

Fine.

It always happens.

The boy knows
what to do.

He goes fishing the same stretch of water he angled
with his father all his life till now.

The beaver ponds shine
like a string of pearls.

It isn't easy to fly-cast a mirror-
finish.

The ponds are silting in.

It always happens.

They turn
into meadows.

The stream is choked with sweet-smelling grasses,
cottonwoods, and willows.

He knows what to do with fifty feet
of line out, shadow-casting.

The loops flash over his head, electric
in the sunlight, as if to illustrate grief, or the hem of a luminous
dress in motion.

Then the tapered line rifles out, and the lead-
wing touches water with no more force than its own tiny weight.

The surface breaks.

They call them rainbows for a reason.

The boy
opens his father's clasp-knife to open the fish.

As he does this
some lint trapped under the blade, like a cottonwood seed from

his father's pocket, falls out and parachutes down to the grass, and suddenly this boy, it always happens, doesn't know what to do anymore.

They Haven't Heard the West Is Over

So that no one should forget, and no one be forgotten— isn't that what graves are for? The road from Tie Siding labors up the ridge like an old man in deep snow, leading the ditch like a mule, like always, making the woods by dark. The timber goes from green to blue on its way to the bone-white Divide.

Off the road there, in the lee of the rise (so that no one should forget), in a mixed patch of evergreen and aspen (so that no one be forgotten), you can barely see the rail fence, a brief enclosure, through the living trees.

Rough stones pried from the ground nearby, these markers bear no names. But I know who is buried here, and who repairs the rails. These folk were pioneers, and are, apart from other people: Ap Worster and his wife so frail he could place his hands wholly around her waist.

She wasn't strong enough to live so far away. Ap climbed a haystack when she died. He lay on his back and cried three days. That was 1910. Someone's girl died in winter, before she had a name. They kept her till the ground thawed. Death had done its work by then, and more.

There are others here that I could name and tell about, but the differences between them now are slight: a balsam tree is growing out of someone, someone is covered by an aspen bough, newly fallen.

Besides, these are not like graves in town that no one should forget. These were meant to be forgotten. Some people never stop wanting to disappear into the mountains. Right now the whole of Wyoming opens its rusty arms to the north, and the road from here keeps going, as if it were going somewhere.

Little Anthem

Cool in brindled shade below the springbox,
Willows muster and fold over
In green vaults
To assemble and reassemble the place
My mother planted watercress
A long time, now, ago.

That deep in green was hers,
Safe from deer and safe from horses.

Shallow water doctors the light,
And the vague silt settles down
Vegetable and feathery
Like the inside of a living eye.
The watercress is a secret floating country,
Its own green flag,

With history.
It's quiet here,

Despite the water's
Small gasps of surprise,
But the noise Ernie raised
Repairing the springbox lid
Was an old man's pissing and moaning
And a glorious hurling about of tools in rage.

Father gave orders to stay clear of Ernie,
Whose meanness came from dying slowly,

But my mother sent me down for watercress.
Above my head, a cat's paw hit the tree.

I knelt and touched the atmosphere
Those numb leaves lived in.
Keeping myself small, I tore up handfuls.
Howling, Ernie sent his hammer arcing.

One of his eyes was made of glass
And it wavered toward me.

What desire
Held me there against which fears?
When my bowl greenly overflowed, I stayed.
When his fury lost its way in sadness, I stayed.
When he set to work again,
I stayed.

And what I stole from him
Was mine.

The Last Man's Club

My grandfather was always sad. Sadly, as a boy, he paddled his canoe along the beautiful Hudson River, which was only then beginning to die. During the first war he was very sad in France because he knew he was having the time of his life. When it was over everyone in America felt like a hero—imagine.

Once a year on Armistice Day, he met with all his friends from the war. They got drunk and recounted the stories of the time when they had thought they were men and the world had seemed entirely possible. They placed empty chairs for certain of the dead, and in the center of the table, a bottle of cognac from France, for the last man of them to drink alone, in honor of the others.

Year after year they gathered to watch each other and themselves disappear, turn into empty chairs. Sooner or later they all were sad. Some of them must have realized they didn't need to join a club for this.

Finally it came down to my grandfather and a man named Oscar Cooper. Neither of them wanted to outlive anyone. They couldn't remember what honor was. When they drank the cognac it didn't taste like anything. They threw the bottle in the river as if they thought it meant that neither of them was alive anymore.

When Cooper died the following year, my grandfather took his rifle out into the yard and fired three shots at the sky. Then he went down to the river and drank himself to sleep. After that he was never sad, not even when the river died.

What Holds Them Apart

In those days they worked from loose stacks to the stationary baler and tied the bales by hand.

                    Lyle's name means *the island,* but he doesn't know that.

                    His hayfield, a peat bog, is the only level ground on this side of the mountain.

                    For a time I was young enough to catch tadpoles in ditches and take them home in mayonnaise jars while all the men were haying.

                    Long afternoons I fished in the creek that runs through Lyle's meadow.

          I knew that water down to the bottom stones.

                    Deep pools were friends.

                    Fingery willows that snagged my hand-tied flies were enemies.

                    Lyle never liked the sound of his name.

         He prefers to work alone.

                    He used to have a family, but they're gone.

                  When he isn't haying he's building things by hand.

            He makes tools to make tools to make things like hay barns and violins and muzzle-loading guns whose barrels he taps, whose triggers, locks, and hammers he forges.

                    That summer he was building a new room on our house.

                    He wanted me to build retaining walls, so he took me down and showed me something about the creek I didn't know.

                                        We shoveled sand
all afternoon.
            You might think cement is what holds the
stones in a wall together.
                        Masons know it's what holds them
apart.
            And mortar is mostly sand from the river.
                                        I couldn't
see why we needed retaining walls—just because there's
no level ground on this side, and you have to notch the
slope to build on.
            I couldn't imagine the mountain as a
slower kind of river.
                    We pried big stones from a knoll
of frost-cracked granite.
                        They were angular, irregular.

You could see the whole Medicine Bow and Laramie Peak from
there.
            We loaded the truck bed till the springs were flat,
and then some.
                    I learned to stagger the seams and fit the
random stones by trying different combinations, as if the
wall were a puzzle with one ideal order that doesn't make
a picture, and whose puzzle-parts weigh fifty pounds each,
so it hurts to change your mind.
                            They never really fit
till you tear them down and build them back in order, with
mortar to hold them apart.
                        I remember remembering a photo-
graph I'd seen of the house Lyle was born in.
                                        It was out

on the flats of eastern Colorado.

Most of the picture was
pale, cloudless sky.

There wasn't a tree or a bump on the
land except that house, which was made of the same dirt
and prairie grass it was lost in.

A house made of earth
that you couldn't see anything from.

Now Lyle, who doesn't
like the sound of his name, which he doesn't know means
the island, is standing on the roof with a hammer in his
right hand.

He wears dark glasses and a painter's cap,
an apron full of nails.

The sun is behind him. I can't
see his face.

I'm hot and tired and I don't understand why we need retaining
walls.

I shade my eyes and see a redtail hawk circling the
deep blue and sun above us.

I'm trying to say the kind of thing
a man would say.

I put down this stone and offer,

*That hawk
up there sure has it easy.*

Lyle doesn't even look up.

He looks
at me.

He pushes the glasses up on his nose and turns back to work.

He says,

Easy, but hungry.